A KEY INTO THE

LANGUAGE OF AMERICA

ALSO BY ROSMARIE WALDROP

PHILIP. *KING* of Mount Hope.

Philip, King of Mt. Hope.
*Print by P. Revere; courtesy of the John Carter Brown Library
at Brown University.*

ROSMARIE WALDROP

A KEY INTO THE
LANGUAGE OF AMERICA

A NEW DIRECTIONS BOOK

Grateful acknowledgment is made to the editors and publishers of magazines
and journals in which sections of this book first appeared: *Avec, Central
Park, Five Finger Review, Mandorla, o.blek, Private, Sonora Review, Sul-
fur,* and *Talisman.*

The book is based on Roger Williams's *A Key Into the Language of America*
of 1643. It also contains quotes from Michel Fardoulis-Lagrange and Claire
Needell.

Book design by Frezzolini Severance, Westerly, Rhode Island
Manufactured in the United States of America
New Directions Books are printed on acid-free paper.
First published as New Directions Original Paperbook 798 in 1994
Published simultaneously in Canada by Penguin Books Canada Limited

Library of Congress Cataloging-in-Publication Data

Waldrop, Rosmarie.
    A key into the language of America / Rosmarie Waldrop.
        p.   cm
    Based on Roger Williams's 1643 book of the same name.
    ISBN 0–8112–1287–4
    1. Williams, Roger, 1604?–1683—Relations with Indians—Poetry. 2.
Indians of North America—Rhode Island—First contact with Europeans—
Poetry.   3. Narragansett Indians—Poetry.   I. Title.
PS3573.A4234K48   1994
811'.54—dc20   94–10503
                                                                CIP

New Directions Books are published for James Laughlin
by New Directions Publishing Corporation
80 Eighth Avenue, New York 10011

FOR HANK HINE

CONTENTS

TABLE OF ILLUSTRATIONS

A KEY

INTO THE

LANGUAGE OF AMERICA,

OR AN

HELP TO THE LANGUAGE OF THE NATIVES IN THAT PART OF AMERICA CALLED

New=England;

TOGETHER WITH BRIEFE OBSERVATIONS OF THE CUSTOMES, MANNERS, AND WORSHIPS, &c. OF THE AFORESAID

NATIVES,

IN PEACE AND WARRE, IN LIFE AND DEATH.

On all which are added,

SPIRITUALL OBSERVATIONS GENERALL AND PARTICULAR, BY THE AUTHOUR, OF CHIEFE AND SPECIALL USE (UPON ALL OCCASIONS) TO ALL THE ENGLISH INHABIT-
ING THOSE PARTS; YET PLEASANT AND
PROFITABLE TO THE VIEW OF
ALL MEN.

By ROGER WILLIAMS,
Of Providence, in New-England.

LONDON.
PRINTED BY GREGORY DEXTER.
1643.

Facsimile of the title page of the 1643 edition of Roger Williams's *A Key into the Language of America* from the *Collections of the Rhode-Island Historical Society, Vol. I,* printed by John Miller, 1827.

Courtesy of Bruce N. Goodsell, Westerly, Rhode Island.

INTRODUCTION

A KEY INTO A KEY

A Key into the Language of America takes its title, chapter
sequence, and many quotations from Roger Williams's book
of 1643 with the same title.

I live in the former territory of the Narragansett Indians, in
Rhode Island, the colony Williams founded as a haven of
religious freedom after he was banished from the theocratic
Massachusetts Bay Colony for his non-conformist opinions.

I was not born here. Like the first settlers, I came from
Europe. I came, expecting strangeness, expecting to be disori-
ented, but was shocked, rather, by my lack of culture shock.
Nothing seemed too different from my native Germany—
except for the Indian place-names. I was at first irritated by
them: my ears could not quite take them in, my eyes were
disoriented by their spelling:

> Aquidneck
> Chepachet
> Cocumscussock
> Misquamicut
> Pascoag
> Pawtucket
> Pawcatuck

Quonochontaug
Woonasquatucket

Then, gradually, I became fascinated with the irritant, the otherness of these names, the strangeness of their music, which alone inscribes the Indian past in the present space. The Narragansett language, not written down, existed only in time and vanished with it.

I turned to Williams's book for a look at this language, for some context around these place names. For a bit more Indian subsoil—or perhaps groundwater—under the soil of American English.

I found something much richer than a primer or phrase-book, though Williams's book is that also: the first extensive vocabulary and study of an Indian language printed in English. Williams had not only

> a constant zealous desire to dive into the Indian lan-
> guage . . . , but a painful Patient spirit to lodge with
> them, in their filthy smoke holes (even while I lived at
> Plymouth and Salem) to gain their tongue . . . and
> could debate with them in a great measure in their
> own Language.[1]

The book is, besides, a sympathetic presentation of Indian customs, again the first I know of. Williams recognized a culture where his compatriots saw only savage otherness.

Roger Williams was a preacher and initially approached the natives as a missionary, undertaking what the Massachusetts Bay and Plymouth colonists had professed as a goal but not

1. Neal Salisbury, *Manitou and Providence: Indians, Europeans, and the Making of New England, 1500–1643*, New York: Oxford University Press, 1982, p. 194.

put into practice: the conversion of the native population to Christianity. "I am no Elder in any church . . . nor ever shall be, if the Lord please to grant my desires that I may intend what I long after, the Natives Soules," he wrote to Governor John Winthrop, in mid-1632.[2]

Williams's Christianity proved perhaps the only hindrance to his anthropological observations; for the Indians' religion disturbed him deeply. He writes:

> I confesse to have most of these their [religious] cus-
> toms by their owne Relation, for after once being in
> their Houses and beholding what their Worship was, I
> durst never bee an eye witnesse, Spectatour, or looker
> on, least I should have been partaker of Sathans Inven-
> tions and Worships, contrary to *Ephes.* 5.11.
>
> [*A Key*, Chapter XXI]

Williams was all the more impressed with the Indians' con-
duct, which seemed to put the Christians to shame—and with-
out the help of divine grace. For, if he was uneasy about the
Indian religion, he was indignant about much of what the colo-
nists were doing. *The Key* is written for them, for his compa-
triots—who immediately misunderstood its intention. They
regarded it as a factual handbook, of great practical use to trad-
ers, missionaries and settlers. As John J. Teunissen and Evelyn
J. Hinz say in the introduction to their 1973 reprint edition:

> Since the conversion of the Indian and trade with him
> were the ostensible reasons for colonization advanced
> by all parties and since the granting of the charter [for

2. *Ibid.*

the Providence Plantations] coincided with the publication of *A Key*, it was only natural for both Williams's supporters and opponents to treat the book as evidence of his success as a colonial agent.[3]

But the original book was not written as a handbook for successful colonization. It was written not only to teach a language, but also to teach a lesson.

Each chapter moves through three stages: through phrase lists and anthropological observations (which often contain ironical comments on the supposedly superior Europeans) to a final moralizing poem. The poem is always introduced with the words "More particular:", marking the importance of the lesson over the factual information preceding it. In these poems, the Indians serve as a mirror held up to the Christians:

> The courteous *Pagan* shall condemne
> *Uncourteous Englishmen,*
> Who live like Foxes, Beares and Wolves,
> Or Lyon in his Den.
>
> Let none sing *blessing* to their soules,
> For that they Courteous are:
> The wild *Barbarians* with no more
> Than Nature, goe so farre:
>
> If Nature's Sons both *wild* and *tame,*
> Humane and Courteous be:
> How ill becomes it Sonnes of God
> To want Humanity?
>
> [*A Key,* Chapter I]

3. John J. Teunissen and Evelyn J. Hinz, ed., *Roger Williams: A Key into the Language of America,* Detroit: Wayne State University Press, 1973, p. 24.

Williams, the Christian, is amazed that the Indians tended to behave better than their Christian counterparts—and that with only "Nature's teaching." One could draw different conclusions from this. But Roger Williams saw the opportunity for a lesson.

The lesson was moral and spiritual. It was also political.

> The Natives are very exact and punctuall in the bounds of their Lands. . . . And I have knowne them make bargaine and sale amongst themselves for a small piece, or quantity of Ground: notwithstanding a sinfull opinion among many that Christians have right to *Heathens* Lands: but of the delusion of that phrase, I have spoke in a discourse. . . .
>
> [*A Key,* Chapter XVI]

The discourse referred to was a treatise written in 1632, which argued that a royal patent did not entitle English colonists to Indian land, that such land had to be purchased from the natives themselves, that it was in fact sinful of both the Crown and the colonists to usurp land from the natives.

One argument of particular interest (reported by the Puritan clergyman John Cotton) is Williams's attack on the doctrine of *vacuum domicilium,* the doctrine that the colonists were entitled to the land because the Indians were not making full use of it. Williams observed that while it was true that the natives cultivated only a small portion of their land, they used all of it for hunting and, for this purpose, regularly burned the underbrush. As Neal Salisbury points out in his book *Manitou and Providence,* this is an argument based not on some abstractions of international law, but on direct ethnographic observation. Williams recognized that Indian hunting and burning were not random activities, but systematic, rational uses of land in the same sense that cultivation was for Europeans.[4]

Williams's recognition that the Indians were making rational and full use of the land was a most unwelcome idea. It challenged the colonists' right to the land they were occupying. It is not surprising that the Boston magistrates had the tract burned. Nor that they considered Williams a dangerous man.

Roger Williams had already attacked the basis of the Puritan theocracy of Massachusetts Bay Colony by advocating the separation of church and state. He held that the civil power of a state could properly have no jurisdiction over the consciences of men, and that an oath could not be administered to an unregenerate man, oaths being a form of worship. Challenging the colonists' title to the land was the last straw. Moreover, as Perry Miller writes, he "thus threatened the very bases of the society at a moment when the possibility of an Anglican invasion to revoke the [Massachusetts] charter and to reduce Massachusetts to conformity with England was real," so that Williams seemed to be playing into the hands of the enemy. Hence, Miller continues, "the state dealt with him as any state must deal with such agitators. The statesmen who exiled him never repented."[5]

In July 1635, Roger Williams was formally tried for his political heresies by the Massachusetts General Court and, when he did not recant, banished from Massachusetts for 300 years. An attempt was made to deport him to England, but he was forewarned and fled to an Indian settlement on the east

4. Salisbury, p. 176 f.
5. Perry Miller, *Roger Williams,* New York: Atheneum, 1966, p. 26.

bank of the Seekonk River, where he bought land from the Indians and founded the settlement he called Providence, "in grateful remembrance of God's merciful providence to him in his distress." He lived by farming and trade with the Indians.

The mirror Roger Williams held up to the colonists in *A Key into the Language of America* was not welcome. Even a hundred years later, when the Massachusetts Historical Society reprinted extracts from *A Key* in 1794 and 1798, the poems and the passages critical of the New English were omitted, as well as phrases expressing Roger Williams's admiration for the Indians. For instance, "omitted from the observation of the Edenic nature of native clothing is the phrase, 'after the patterne of their and our first Parents.'"[6] What was reprinted was a utilitarian guide to customs and vocabulary.

I live in Roger Williams's territory. I was born in 1935, the year Williams's 300-year banishment officially ended. I was born "on the other side," in Germany. Which was then Nazi Germany. I am not Jewish. I was born on the side of the (then) winners. I was still a child when World War II ended with the defeat of the Nazis. I immigrated to the US, the country of the winners, as a white, educated European who did not find it too difficult to get jobs, an advanced degree, a university position. I can see myself, to some extent, as a parallel to the European settlers/colonists of Roger Williams's time (though I did not think God or destiny had set the country aside for me as a virgin garden). Like Roger Williams, I am ambivalent about my position among the privileged, the "conquerors."

But am I among them? I am white and educated. I am also a poet and a woman. A poet, in our days, is regarded as rather

6. Teunissen & Hinz, p. 25.

a marginal member of society, whose social usefulness is in doubt. As a woman, I do not figure as conqueror in the shell game of archetypes, but as conquered. A "war bride." As a woman, I also have no illusions about the Indian societies. They were far from ideal.

I live in Roger Williams's territory. By coincidence and marriage I share his initials. I share his ambivalence.

In the shell game of archetypes, the conquered (people or land) is always female:

> No more had Columbus landed, the flower once
> ravished . . .[7]

The colonization of America put the very "male" Indian culture in the position of the conquered female, part of the land that was considered there to be "taken." I can identify with both sides of the conflict and am ambivalent about each side.

In 1635, Roger Williams found the Narragansetts at the height of their power, in a strong, if not dominant, intertribal position. They had not been decimated by the great smallpox epidemic of 1616–19 and, according to estimates, numbered some thirty thousand.

For a while, Williams was able to arbitrate between them and the colonists. He was able to induce the Narragansetts to ally themselves with the English against the Pequots. But he was traveling to England (ironically, to secure a charter for Rhode Island) when the Narragansetts lost their fight with the Mohegans. The Narragansett sachem Miantonomi, who had called for the tribes to unite in common cause against the

7. William Carlos Williams, *In the American Grain,* New York: New Directions, 1933, p. 7.

English, was captured, turned over to the Commissioners of the United Colonies and executed at their behest by the Mohegan chief Uncas.

Roger Williams was there, but unable to arbitrate when another Narragansett sachem, Metacomet or King Philip, rose up against the English in 1675. Williams saw the Narragansetts defeated in the Great Swamp Fight, King Philip's head hung up as a public display in Boston, the Narragansett tribe devastated, and most of them indentured into service in colonial homes.

Indenture was better than being sold into slavery, but it helped erode Indian customs. By the middle of the eighteenth century, the Indians were dressing in European style. By 1800, the Narragansett language was dead.

Except in place names:

> Conimicut
> Matunuck
> Meshanticut
> Namquit
> Poppasquash
> Saugatucket
> Usquepaug
> Weekapaug

And in our time?

Grave sites on Conanicut Island, skeletons buried in fetal position, facing southwest, in the direction of their paradise.

Narragansett stone masons, carpenters, factory workers. A few owners of restaurants or gift shops, managers or masonry contractors. "Achievement in professional employment has reached the level of the master's degree in nursing. Yet, most Narragansett do not go beyond high school in education, and many have dropped out of high school."[8]

But there has been much restoration of Indian practices. In 1934, only one of the elected tribal officials listed in *The Narragansett Dawn,* a local Indian monthly, has an Indian name; by 1950, all of them do. However, with the Narragansett language dead, "the Indians who wanted to have Indian names had the choice of picking names out of Roger Williams's 1643 volume or creating English word-names that conveyed something of the personality of the person."[9]

We have come full circle. Now, Roger Williams's book is for the Indians.

And for me. Besides giving me a glimpse of a vanished language and culture, *A Key* has given me the form of this work.

In parallel to Roger Williams's anthropological passages, the initial prose section of each of my chapters tries to get at the clash of Indian and European cultures by a violent collage of phrases from Williams with elements from anywhere in my Western heritage. I try to enact the confrontation of the two cultures by juxtapositions, often within a single sentence. Roger Williams's voice will be recognized by its archaic syntax and vocabulary printed in boldface. There is also an additional tension between the values of the seventeenth-century settlers, "Saints," "Pilgrims," and my own, which are not only

8. Ethel Boissevain, *The Narragansett People,* Indian Tribal Series/Phoenix, 1975, p. 93.
9. *Ibid.,* p. 92.

secular, but also informed by twentieth-century hindsight as to the long-range destruction inherent in the settlers' struggle to survive.

To reinforce the theme of conquest and gender, every chapter adds a narrative section in italics, in the voice of a young woman, ambivalent about her sex and position among the conquerors.

Every chapter also has its word list and final poem. These play across both themes.

Unlike Roger Williams's, my word lists are not of practical use, but explore the language context (rather than cultural context) of the chapter titles. The words in the lists may be suggested by the sound of a title word (e.g. "fission" in the chapter on fishing) or may play across its semantic field ("interlacing" and "contagion" in the chapter on "Relations of Consanguinity"). Many lists explore compounds of title words (busy[body], [body]guard, [body]snatcher in Chapter VII) or grammatical elements like suffixes ([season]able, [season]ing in Chapter X). There are also some Narragansett phrases.

All in all, my book could be called an immigrant's take on the heritage and complex early history of my adopted country. Or perhaps a dive into the waters of the Moosup and Pawtuxet Rivers, of Mishnock, Ninigret, Pasquiset, Watchaug, Wesquage, and Yawgoog Ponds.

"The Figure of the Indians' Fort
or Palizado in New England" from
John Underhill, *News from America*, London, 1638.
Courtesy of the John Carter Brown Library at Brown University.

A KEY INTO THE

LANGUAGE OF AMERICA

CHAPTER I

SALUTATIONS

Are of two sorts and come immediately before the body. The pronunciation varies according to the point where the tongue makes contact with pumice found in great quantity. This lends credence, but no hand. Not so entirely Narragansett, the roof of the mouth. Position of hand or weapon conventional or volcanic formation.

Asco wequassunnúmmis. Good Morrow.
> sing
> salubrious
> imitation
> intimate

*I was born in a town on the other side which didn't want me in so many. All streets were long and led. In the center, a single person had no house or friends to **allay excessive sorrowe.** I, like other girls, forgot my name in the noise of traffic, opening my arms more to measure their extension than to offer embrace.*

the Courteous Pagan
barefoot and yes
his name laid down
as dead
one openness
one woman door
so slow in otherwise
so close

CHAPTER II

OF EATING
AND ENTERTAINMENT

Indian corne, boiled with free will and predestination is a dish **exceeding wholesome** if taken through the mouth. Their words, too, fit to eat. And crow. A mark of "cadency." Similarly, an eye devouring its native region must devote special attention to its dialect. **Where they have themselves and their wives risen to prepare.** Against initiative of elements, against white bodies, against coining of new words: Tobacco. Unsuccessful.

Mishquockuk.
Red Copper Kettle.
cycle
chain
for thought

I began my education by walking along the road in search of the heroic. I did not think to ask the way to the next well. Wilderness like fear a form of drunkenness or acting like a boy. The ground begins to slip. Rhythm of swallows seen from below. It is a strange truth that remains of contentment are yet another obstacle.

> the spelling in my mother's recipes
> explains
> why she gave birth to me
> and in the greatest heat
> should feed
> on me
> all flesh considered
> as a value

CHAPTER III

CONCERNING SLEEPE
AND LODGING

They will sleepe without the doores, above sea-level, with fragments and English translations. The night too long ago for architecture. Rocks shifting in the river-beds, escaping recognition, the vigilance of leaves. When the swelling of a tenor voice is (for want of theology) observed by a procession of closed eyes they wake up young and know they've been.

in
over
out
walk

*Later I played under highway bridges to make room for strangers. A smell of concrete and mud, acrid as of sexual transactions. Ripples on puddles. Faintly foetal. On the periphery of more private weather, I tried to adjust to Dutch trumpets and **fire instead of bedclothes**. This was inevitable if I wanted to learn to imitate consciousness.*

the powers of
Wunnakukkússaqùaum
pale flesh
You Sleep Much
restored to take imagination
by surprise
out by the roots of dream
an empty
promise
lodged against me

CHAPTER IV

OF THEIR NUMBERS

Without the help of Wall Street, how quick they are in casting up inalienable numbers. We do not have them. With help of hybrid corn instead of Europe's pens or poisons. Edge of ingenuity, between numb and nimble, forest or frigid wave before it crashes. Let it be considered whether a split providence or separate encystments in their own minds have taught them. Or concentration, its circular surface. What's called **arithmaticke**. A riddle on which matter rests.

Pawsuck. Of The Masculine Gender.
Pâwsuck. One Of The Feminine Gender.

Pâwsuck with time to dawdle, to cultivate lucidity and metric structure. Yet did not play by numbers. Too many messengers that do not speak. A bowel movement every day and one war every generation. I feared becoming an object too boring for my bones to hold up, however clumsily.

nostalgia figured
in bruised shins
and loss
loss of eternity
in triplicate
such that my knees
could come apart
and tell
their seeds

CHAPTER V

OF THEIR RELATIONS OF CONSANGUINITIE AND AFFINITIE, OR, BLOOD AND MARRIAGE

They hold it red and wear it on their skin, a bond prey to contact and bylaws, that when one dies they will adopt degrees of singular. 'Tis **common for a brother** to pry a mass of igneous rock concealing fatherless children. Their virgins are prized in ornamental openwork which requires service of four fingers or more. Intrusions in the art(eries). Hardened with suspense. To each his own. There is no inner stain or stream carrying oxygen and guilt. But a father was known to **take so grievously.** I am obliged to tell that **hee hat cut and stob'd him-selfe.**

> interlacing
> contagion
> curdling
> letting
> pressure
> thirsty

My sister. Had closed her eyes and strayed into the hidden monoxide of the highway, disregarding maternal grief. Once she had taken this distance I cleared a level of fog as dense as semen and paused, indifferent to the conflicts of common descent.

born hard heroic upright
to tear against
the wick of natural affections
of clothed sleep

when one so similar has disappeared
we must build shells
to make it safe to have a self

CHAPTER VI

OF THE FAMILY AND BUSINESSSE OF THE HOUSE

A solemne word, family, that no one trained to explore celestial mobilities would try to hinder. Not even a stranger. Above genus and below order. Covered with chestnut bark. They stow their families along diagonal axes and put their eggs in baskets, pigs in pokes. Prefer the movement of planets or buffalo to European **coat-men,** identifiable strains to city planning even when applied to lexical items. **Wetuomémese. A Little House. Which women live apart in,** the time of their exhaustive volume. Of the roundest. The aperture secured, so no eruptions may crash out of proportion. Or **long poles** on the off side of finance. Which commonly the men erect. Long neck and body. A longer house with a last stand.

> the other
> and its head
> sleep has no
> of mirth
> the fall

A procession, a river of people, the whole town crossed into exaltation to subject the body to their rites of candle and flame, cries and bewailing, morning and evening. Could I withdraw from such offering. I was not innocent enough to expect an end to hostility and housemaid's knee. A faulty birth no guarantee of entrance. Nature the more ruthless in getting back its chemicals. I rushed my headlong into it and found I made no splash. It would take a different kind of water to quench my long terror.

No one comes ignorant
among corners and stones
carrying beans
and a tune
and child besides

a stranger's
tongue they must yet do not
know
will twist their lullaby
their child their hand-me-down
their gums their genes their lovingly

CHAPTER VII

OF THEIR PERSONS AND PARTS OF BODY

Great bunch of **hayre** raked from darkness, yet as organized a physical substance as **sober English.** And can be photographed. In the brain, the proportion of quick apprehension to arable not less deep a structure than distinguished from limbs and labor or the central part of a document distinguished from title, nave, garment, soundbox, or viscosity. Though childbirth will force christianity down the ladder into fighting units: women never forgive unparted flesh.

busy
guard
snatcher

I was shorn of illusion and impulse, though with a sorry knife, before touching amorous form. Where were my eyes? My heart was good and went to meet that difficult unfolding. Nudity in danger. All manner of man and of what bigness chased me to the bottom of my ignorance, desolately sublimating the fewness of wishes. Inexact report.

My long blue birth
snatched
from what sense of deed
what horizontal sleep
whereas
a virgin marriageable
can slip
like fog in anywhere

CHAPTER VIII

OF DISCOURSE AND NEWES

Tidings on condition, a corresponding sign to sound which our geologists have discolored toward the vanishing point. Echo off yore, their preoccupation: **if white men speake true** or only to disturb the air. Even living in translation **they deliver themselves** at arm's length with emphatic purpose according to stress and position and sometimes alongside it. The message, slowed down by change of climate, becomes obsolete. **And understand not** that a tongue must keep in consonant motion to cover up its fork.

                     print
                    worthy

Pannóuwa awàun, awaun keesitteóuwin.	Some Body Hath Made This Lie.

*Too long I took clockwork as a model instead of follow-
ing the angle my inclinations make with the ground. **Why
speake I not,** I should have asked, counting on articula-
tion of sound forms in waiting. The restless oscillations
stripped me of more mythic aspirations and left my mus-
cles mendicant, destiny manifest, skeleton without closet.
When it is here, when it is come, alone or in a crowd, the
moment always a matrix of terrible and stupid. My
tongue so tied. To mother. Never as clear as when
straight impulse bends back into curve.*

comes as
bait
where speaking
is still possible
**the messenger
runs swiftly** till
no
matter how
he can't forget

CHAPTER IX

OF THE TIME OF THE DAY

how high the sun
how ceaseless centigrades
how irritation systems
Nippúckis. Smoke Troubled Me.
how to the north and west
how measure mayhem
how along the Mississippi
how taking plains
how foregone concussion

capsule
consuming
deposit
exposure
honored
lapse

I wouldn't give him. Big time traded for small syn-chronicities seen from below. Coincidence of confusion and unrest. "Wild" corresponded less to aggression than women's lips. Insomnia was long ago. With everything reduced to adult silence charged with local shadow play and cloudbursts. What was happening in my organism belied the flags for sunrise. An anorexic memory served to release promises around the clock. A drop of blood there to be seen.

                    the speech of light
                    curled in a leaf
                    so in broad time
                    the make of mind
                    takes off the sky
                    beyond the sphere
                    of eye yet not
                    the frame around
                    the body

CHAPTER X

OF THE SEASON
OF THE YEERE

They have thirteen moneths and are content to settle for that many. The courage to grow organs in reply to want, the way a giraffe stretches her neck to mounting advantage. If seasons can force the day around the sun there is no end to threshold or shedding skin. The chief difficulty with nature's outline yields hand-held exposures such as **Tashecautúmmo. How Many Years Since** fatal expression, since semantics, since influence.

able
ing

Made to sleep on the balcony, I tried to lord it over the kids still playing on the sidewalk. My space eked out by height, with family prejudice to back me up. With acute daring I dropped a tin box the way you drop a plumbline down into sleep causing rings to widen out until a boy stuck his finger into the gob of spittle I had carefully placed inside. The shore fell into ruins.

> machinery in place behind
> hurt sharp
> enough to trace
> into the wiring of psychology
> a risk of
> membranes
> undercuts the alibi

CHAPTER XI

OF TRAVELL

What paths their swift of foot have cut in history and philosophy, with distinct genital extensions toward the Great Plains. A feeling of wings in the air will move understanding. So vast, distressed, undone, in search of company to **take tobacco and discourse.** Whirl of environs, exaggerations and limping, lamenting lingua franca.

> **Mayúo?**
> **Is There A Way?**
> there is no way
> unscathed
>
> ogue
> agent
> er

*Sticks and stones and swamps and howling wilderness, or
inside a patient garden and ability to behave: intrepid
waiting. Sad career. Crisp choice. Methodical muscles.
Learning too slowly to be always in motion. Because of
my uterine heritage an inner heat pushed my knees to-
ward desire and superhuman effort at the risk of getting
lost and needing **the succor of savages.***

as if but once
they think they live
and without shoes into
**the contrey's
bowels**

my
arms twisted
from birth
to stay
inside and add
it up to zero

CHAPTER XII

CONCERNING THE HEAVENS
AND HEAVENLY LIGHTS

Which they adore, above acknowledging colonization. The stellar pallor attending powers shot madly from their spheres, the sky all over the earth, heaving its divine dimensions. If quickened circulation acts upon our thoughts, the moon so old it sets in full proportion. A light that does not slap you in the face, but raises nouns like navigation and transcendence. Nothing strange in pigment (black) that does not feed on side-stars obtained by imperfect combustion. Rocks. Meteorites. Great Western Railway.

opalescent
celestial
celibacy

*An inner heat, an inflammation, predicting intimacies to hurt your eyes. Expanse of bodies, heavenly, observed on **lying in the fields.** Frequent occasion. And measured by their angle **much observed in motion,** like the tin box tossed, sure curve belonging only to itself. Parabolas of the inanimate, these very children will throw stones.*

toward sunset
the uninvited guests
have guns
and written off
red skin

they (mis)
take territory
for imperative

CHAPTER XIII

OF THE WEATHER

It may bee wondred why, New England being 12° neerer to the Sun, reality is yet in doubt. Some parts of winter act as lens owing to long reach as the **Nor West wind comes** under varying conditions and over loads of snow. If, when thin, the air unites the tribal factions, and a long vowel, more cold than overcast, **runnes about starke naked,** a climatic change occurs. American enough is all they know of atoms. Atmosphere windward like sexual feeling and as unpredictable, thick and vapory.

                    beaten
                    bound
                    cock
                    eye
                    under

My spittle overflowed literal expectations and was caught in flagrant light. Giggles sapped my resolve to leave home for unwobbling hyperbole. Inner darkness. Euphoric entropy. In a mixture of panic and mistaken gender I went West, intending the milky way. Common error.

no one
an island
warmer than continents
would
in sharpest hemisphere
would mobilize
big masculine history
on tap

CHAPTER XIV

OF THE WINDS

Accounts for eight cardinalls flying out of context though not explaining **the accurate division of the compasse** or where to blow. A motion that now buffets, now cools, has passed, more fertile in another period, the way tradition places God to **the Southwest of pleasingest** and passive.

What Think You When The Wind Blows From The East?

> burn
> fall
> lass
> rose
> row
> ow

The wind from a past only recently mine drove racial discrimination between the poles of my life and divided the city into usage and flooding. My family's limbs dispersed in reciprocities, but rejoined as if emerging out of water, more whole than before, but still bone-white as we lay on our bloated stomachs, as if already dead.

here
the wind
will be tomorrow
a constant disquisition
into the secret of
velocity
while men grow small
within their skin
tongue tied
into another language

CHAPTER XV

OF FOWLE

Auchaûi. Gone Afowling. The crows eat up the sky, and the Indians hear an airplane rumble in their eardrums. Estranged, the feathered sacred, the aspirates of prophecy. **There be millions ready to devour corn** as soon as it appears out of the mouth and falls on careless ears and general conclusions. **Unto them** a pass on history **be well resembled.** Long proof, short fire. Hence so **marvellous desirous** of the English guns and melancholy carriage of the body.

> eagle
> turkey
> partridge
> cormorant
> **Ptowewushánnick.**
> **They are fled.**

I distrusted men. Their bonds with artificial light too close to guarantee a chance of flight. Sometimes, in the lean after-season, their image was twice the distance of the mirror and as pure as the lag between me and my body. I feared the slow pendulum. Steep economic postures hardened to plain absence of imagination. Easily swayed, I constructed kites that floated along the woods, swift messengers of itching ease, of irrigation behind the eyes.

A man who's only
man
may be cut off
from half the world
alleged cause and effect
like the atmosphere
of certain planets
totally opaque

CHAPTER XVI

OF THE EARTH AND THE FRUITS THEREOF

They are exact and punctual in the bounds of property and expectation, but do not admit **Christian rights to Heathens lands.** More densely seeded with disaster. Predictions have been found on paths familiar to the foot. **The women hoe and weede and hill and gather in fruites of the field** and forehead. But though their legs are firmly planted in the ground they do not yield a harvest other than decay. Radiation theory immensely fruitful. The men **not bound to help,** but of a sudden not so big, in turn plowed under, weeded out.

> inconsolable
> succulent
> sphere
> altered
> appendages

Under a show of pink and white, fieldglasses revealed sensual movement which my reserve did not forestall. Nor going to seed. What was the secret of holsters, near-sighted daring, tools between legs? Who went from coast to coast, but stayed always on top with semicircular canals for balance? My antagonism dissolved into the illusion that I was one of them, consenting to slow harm.

if I say come
the siren
will also scream from the police car
as when fields
are to be broken up
all terms are
physical

CHAPTER XVII

OF BEASTS

Netasûog. Cattell. Is the name the Indians give tame beasts, yea as distinguished from their women they keep coiled to the right of the saddle. Black foxes haunt their syntax, not to be snared by lasso or lariat, as everything they cannot comprehend, e.g. deducing of identity from missing rib. Or the beaver, **faire streames** dammed up by him who **sits drie in his chambers,** indifferent to the wheel and other methods of translation. **The termination "suck" is common and therefore added** to our English animals.

> **Cowsuck.**
> **Gôatsuck.**
> **Pigsuck.**
> **Hógsuck.**

*The end of adolescence. Porous to the touch. Dry beds
revealing all that had been drowned. Raw animal spirits
and hand-operated cranks. Rapid motor response cutting
rival kites out of the blank sky. I wondered to what end
these steps and chances taken. Circumstance in place of
instinct. Would uphill follow on uphill, succession of
hopes pawned to always the same anatomical structure?*

    or mouth on mouth
    as it moves
    then tracking back behind
    the nerve
    though without clear
    direction into prey

CHAPTER XVIII

OF THE SEA

A site of passage, of dreadful to move on, of depth between. A native **will take his hatchet** to the Latin of daily life (without postulating long neighborhood or early development) **and burn and hew until he has launched** his morphological innovation on the water. Great transport of bodies, some carrying thirty, forty men. High surface motion, endless, endless. Close resemblance of heavy swell and bewildered, brackish and overwhelming. Heave out hell and high water, yet the future all at sea. **They shall be drowned, the Sea comes in too fast upon them.**

> bed
> biscuit
> cucumber
> farer
> mstress
> nce
> scape
> son

Against the threat of frigidity, I sought out thermal cures which brought me contact with short hair, gratitude, parts called private and more or less so. Without these unidentical skins, masts might have snapped and left me lying right underneath the sky. But my flesh close up was pale and terrified my lover.

a verb
tense beyond
my innermost dark thoughts
but holds
no water
no more than swimmers see
beyond displacement
in exchange

CHAPTER XIX

OF FISH AND FISHING

Rising from sleep teeming with cod, bass, mackerel, salmon, whale and **Kaúposh. Sturgeon.** Yet a native **for the goodness of it will not furnish the English** with the praise they're fishing for. A hook in the throat. Cold eye on the scales. More of commerce than blind allegory. Some English **have begun to salt** as against native smoke the harsh reality. The soul eludes the bait. **Machàge. I have caught none.** Only puns, in **nets they set thwart** drowsy rivers in perfect passive voice, which will be shelled before the next May flowering. Explosive sky.

> fission
> fissile
> fiscal
> whistle
> risk

It was more in retrospect that net results seemed fishy. True, I had swallowed the most intimate head of a cold-blooded vertebrate. Then recollected tranquillity to counteract convulsive laughter. Which might fault me, like any Eve, with expulsion from paradise, or simply lack of hooks. But I was careful not to reveal my age or other unsure passage through the body.

two-chambered hearts
or even more alone
big English will
devour little fish
length of
tooth twice as natural
as equal opportunity

CHAPTER XX

OF THEIR NAKEDNESSE AND CLOTHING

They have a two-fold nakednesse they scan for traces of the self, for differences more deeply seated than between two stools. For though they wear a beast skin yet they are devoid of shame, concealment or disguise. Discrepancy of law pins **little aprons** on their females right from birth, the hairless genitive of price, to frighten off imagination. **Their second nakednesse** unsheathes a lack of foliage, but a few plant names cannot disturb the general conclusion as velvet can with us.

> scantily
> nether
> nor
> on
> opaque

Seeing my shadow on the grass I tried to contain it, like my body, in proper limits. As I had been taught. Also, that nothing, for a woman, is worth trying, except to condense feelings into local ornament. My temper was gloomy, covered with pimples and past secrets, but above sea level. I killed the moment with my hurry to get out of it.

        that if defined by
        feather
        or single organ
        incontinent transplants
        can't undermine our greed
        it's for the birds to flock
        a semblance
        of together

CHAPTER XXI

OF RELIGION, THE SOULE

They won't deny **Englishman's God made English men,** but not the God that made them Indians or the fine discriminations of the subjunctive mood. **They branch their Godhead into many** to attenuate its purpose, just as the possibility of science has diffused coincident quantums of parallel intensity. Upward of 37 names (**Squáuanit. The Women's God.**) suggest that excellence fills every place, so even Europeans could penetrate pregnancy along with fatherhood and fixed abodes. Their soul is twofold like their nakedness. **Cowwéwonck,** from sleep, the time it operates. **Michachunck, in a higher notion, is of affinity with looking glasse or cleere resemblance,** a discernment that returns perception through the hollows of the body and deduces light.

solace
solstice
solemn
solfege
soluble

*Less for reasons of conscience than bad breath I ejected
my lover and sent him back home to teenage acne, to lick
his scars in a narrowed empire, to stroke his continence.
But I could not muster the required indifference. I ached
and tacitly tried to reestablish relations with his bruises.
He had already dug deeper into his hurt, and **his soul
wandered restlesse abroad.***

> that when you die
> **the soul goes West**
> is called perspective and describes
> the weather in a past intense
> with curtains drawn
> to higher aspirations

CHAPTER XXII

OF THEIR GOVERNMENT AND JUSTICE

Caunoúnicus, the elder Sachim, far removed from probability, lets his word stand upon the injury received, his inference more angular against the motivation. The sun also. Hardens. You cannot tell by looking at the sky that breaking laws must take place in the matrix of everyday thought, not runaway amplification. Hence the Sachim either **beats or whips or puts to death with his owne hand** and foot since verse, too, is a form of government. There were 20-odd broken jaws given birthplace and enough (Eu)rope for hanging.

> juggle
> juggernaut
> jugular
> juvenile
> juxtapose

Did I only imagine people pointing fingers at me? No matter that I placed myself dead-center in their discomfort, they picked up the scent, whereas my lover was allowed ritual gestures even in the most traditional frame. If I had an aptitude for growing old, would I find objects worth my guile?

dear reader, I've transgressed
beyond the pale into
yet whiter shades
and all
the elements lie
evenly in periods

CHAPTER XXIII

OF MARRIAGE

Flesh, considered as cognitive region, as opposed to undifferentiated warmth, is called woman or wife. **The number not stinted, yet the Narragansett (generally) have but one.** While diminutives are coined with reckless freedom, the deep structure of the marriage bed is universally esteemed even in translation. **If the woman be false** to bedlock, **the offended husband will be solemnly avenged,** arid and eroded. He may remove her clothes at any angle between horizontal planes.

> mar
> marrow
> mutual
> convenience
> settlement

My lover was ready to overcome all manner of difficulty,
but baffled by my claims to equality and clean towels.
Even with the night between us, neither side would give
up its position and prerogatives. We waited for a change
of weather to reopen hostilities.

> harmony prestabilized
> is turning on its
> axe to grind
> to halt
> to bind
> to fault
> the speed can't be sustained
> even in constant
> rotation
> through periods of waxing and weaning

CHAPTER XXIV

CONCERNING THEIR COYNE

Indians are ignorant of Europe's Coyne yet call it Monéash and notice changes in the price of beaver, somnambulism and songs of myself. Their own is either white, which they call **Wompam,** or black, **Suckáuhock,** made of shellfish and twice as valuable, **hung about the neck** instead of our millstones. **They bring down all their sorts of furs** and trade them for the wish to live, the wish to die, the wish to kill, the wish to be had.

cuneiform
coiffure
coney

I learned that my face belonged to a covert system of exchange since the mirror showed me a landscape requiring diffidence, and only in nightmares could I find identity or denouement. At every street corner, I exaggerated my bad character in hopes of being contradicted, but only caused an epidemic of mothers covering their face while exposing private parts.

legal and tender
a condition called
darling dear or **Netop**
which might as well purchase emotion
as yield interest in
I must explain my body
does not differ

CHAPTER XXV

OF BUYING & SELLING

Amongst themselves they trade great plains of experience for intense feelings **and sometimes come 10, 20 in a company** to seduce the English accents and syntactic peculiarities. **They have some who follow onely making of Bowes and Arrowes;** some follow fishing, hunting; some, classical models. They are **marvailous subtle** and suspect **the English labor to deceive them.** This establishes a bond removing immediate to nothing. **There is not a sorry Howe, Hatchet, Knife or rag of cloth in all America** but has thus come under suspicion and over **the dreadfull Ocean.**

licence
liquor
should
selvage
by and large
by-blow

I traded my overblown ideas for sexual euphoria though I knew getting rid of prejudices would make me fall into some other puddle. The pronoun "I" may be an automatic figure, but the unavowable openings of my body grew larger in response to secret pressures and claimed to be my mind.

> if the dark quarries inner caves
> the sexual act takes on
> a sheen of purchase
> the difference of invasion
> and exodus obscured by labor
> showing its (base) mettle
> rather than coining words:
> **Cuppáimish. I Will Pay You.**
> From the English, even though
> **Cosaúmawem. You Aske Too Much.**

CHAPTER XXVI

OF DEBTS & TRUSTING

They are desirous to come into debt and have bequeathed the habit. **Nowemacaûnash nitteaùquash. I Was Faine to Spend My Money in My Sicknesse is a common and, they think, most satisfying answer** since promises applied to parts of speech have no effect, but a priest's pocket conjures paralysis, convulsions, detritus, and death. In any case, narrow debts cannot offset the introduction of the number zero or opaque treaties of which no word can be deciphered.

> anatomy
> symmetry
> tilt
> expected
> rust

I did not know if my desire to escape cash-and-carry was strong enough to eliminate the platitudes of gender identity or the crowds under my eyelids. I was stuck in a periodicity I supposedly share with Nature, but tired of making concessions to dogs after bones.

I offered sleeplessness
in payment of my debts
but might as well have counted
on my fingers
unlike exposure to harm
the possibilities
of keeping warm not infinite

CHAPTER XXVII

OF THEIR HUNTING

First they pursue their game in grammatical components when **they drive the woods before them.** Secondly, they hunt by traps. Thirdly, by nested, multi-branching constructions. If this is correct it is evidence that organization of memory goes beyond its trivial finite size even if a deer caught in complex variables **lies prey to ranging wolves** who, **at their first devouring, rob the Indian of neere halfe** his take and, in their second greedy meal, of all his land.

Nanówwussu.	It is leane.
Wauwunnockôo.	It is fat.
Weékan.	It is sweet.
Machemóqut.	It smells ill.

Relative appeasement and again intimate with every sin-
gle detail of one man's body. Even though the notion of
marriage had broadened people seemed intent on am-
bushing my love. I must resort to boredom and ruse. A
controversy between. I anticipated much return of the
same but preferred to sniff his armpits.

I must explain my sex
for all its stubbornness
is female
and was long haunted, diligently,
by confusions of habit
and home, time and
the Western world

CHAPTER XXVIII

OF THEIR GAMING

Their public Games, whether cards (**rushes**), dice or football, are self-embedded by the hundreds, for which there is no explanation. **They lie under the trees in a mixture of devotions** and conditioned reflex and will stake their hand or tilt of head (if single persons). **Toward Harvest they set up a Qunnèkamuck or Long House** where they dance inside an innate distance **prepared with money, coats, small breeches,** to give the poor, to creep into thought, to quicken the heart.

> mirror
> fire
> doctor
> fool
> doll

I played the games of ordinary bodies, but my mother still raged to rearrange my memory circuits. Although it is impossible to move fast without gaining weight, I suffered from indecision to the point of giving it free rein. It is then I became lucid and saw phantom equalities evaporate into hope of separate microscopes.

to see your body fold
into a small spot in my skull
just as I'm coiled within
a single organ
a necessary part
of the material world

CHAPTER XXIX

OF THEIR WARRE

Surplus valor comes as messenger and heaves ambush. **Shóttash. Shot. A word made from English though their guns come from the French.** A third arm. Liable to sudden deviation. Then he has against him copious and pathetic voiced explosives to **kindle the flame of wrath** of which **no man knowes how farre** it will branch to the right. A wager on who drew the first bow, on how many slain, the barking of a dog.

> predestination
> desert
> storm
> disability
> **Npúmmuck. I am shot.**

Year of parades. Celebrating exploits unsuited to my con-
stitution. As if every move had to be named expansion,
conquest, trinity, and with American intonation. The
traces of the push across this continent and others no less
flagrant yesterday, but now enlarged with profit and con-
sequence. Our own private ceremony hardly enacted
when it was all already over. Close up, my flesh was dark,
a dead end. My terrified lover left me. For his own like-
ness.

I worried about capture
in wars nobody hears of
a prisoner
in my own genitals
that sum me up to some
my **deep-down-in-the-forest**
my troubled
my self the self of others

CHAPTER XXX

OF THEIR PAINTINGS

1. **They paint their garments**
2. **their faces in warre**
3. color of thought to lacking object
4. **both men and women for pride**
5. closely adherent
6. applies psychology to vanishing point

poly
para
spectrum
structure
raindrop
rage
wavelength

I used iodine to paint my wound, a geometrical design interwoven with collison and conflict. Line securing or towing a boat. A motivation to swell. Or scream in the face of immediate, useless nakedness. In spite of having, without restraint, chosen the wrong role models I have female parts and cultivate outward behavior.

thinking develops
out of the negative

the vacuum abhorred
by nature
is fertile (variables
perspectives, paper money)

refinanced memory
washes white

CHAPTER XXXI

OF SICKNESSE

The Indians' misery appeares they have no physick other than knives in empty air, whereas statistics spread from East to West. When their tongue sticks to the palate, threatened with cessation, they enter a scar-map to sweat out their geography and civic spirit till they almost are themselves and **runne into the Brook.** To wash a different body into their lives.

nasal
velar
labial
guttural
fricative
invasive

Heavy thighs prevent the deformation of desire even
while running great distances. I was determined to track
down my faithless lover, all the while observing local
customs, e.g. dead leaves filling up a space of vacant time.
A great mass of water gathered inside my head without
breaking, which made it difficult to bring forth thought.

        or to say
        the innermost curve
        where music within music proves
        absence of external antecedents
        though even metal may be hampered
        by fatigue
        at this point
        of the instep

CHAPTER XXXII

OF DEATH AND BURIAL

He that hath death in his house **blackes his face.** Soot clotted with tears and gaping with vowels. **They abhorre to mention the dead by the name** sealed into their lips, the bleeding stump of their tongues. **Sachimaûpan. He That Was Prince Here** is wrapped in wailing, in flexion, in hands before the face, in smaller and smaller particles. Perspective unsettled by chemical methods. They bury sideways **the mat he died on, the dish he ate from,** the empty regions of his body, and sometimes hang his shadow upon the next tree which none will touch but suffer to rot.

> occlude
> occult
> orthodox
> haphazard
> obsolete
> irreparable

Solitude in heat. I resented my lover turning his back on me for other mournful realities. Though each crossing of space casually implicates the flesh, attraction increasing faster than distance diminishes, I found myself alone among the rubble of love. I had finally reached the center of the city. It was deserted, in ruins, as useless as my birth and as permanent a site of murder.

              a hitch in time
              then the world changed
              then there was no memory
              then life could not
              be understood forward
              or backward

"A Map of New England" from John Foster's *A Narrative of the Troubles with the Indians in New England*, Boston, 1677.
Courtesy of the John Carter Brown Library at Brown University.

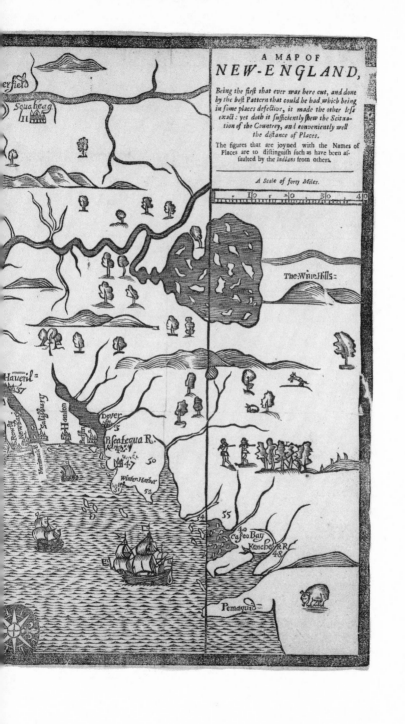

A MAP OF
NEW-ENGLAND,

*Being the first that ever was here cut, and done
by the best Pattern that could be had, which being
in some places defective, it made the other less
exact: yet doth it sufficiently shew the Scitua-
tion of the Countrey, and conveniently well
the distance of Places.*

*The figures that are joyned with the Names of
Places are to distinguish such as have been as-
saulted by the Indians from others.*

A Scale of forty Miles.

10   20   30   40

The Wine Hills

erfield
Squaheag
II

Hauerill
57

Salisbury
Haukton
Rowly
Newbery
Merimack
Dover
Exeter
B. Seafequa R.
43.4
York
47   50
Winter Harbor
52
54   55

Caseo Bay
Kenebek R.
48

Pemaquid